a week at the beach

100 life-changing things
you can do by the seashore

jim and joanne hubal

marlowe & company
new york

A WEEK AT THE BEACH: *100 Life-Changing Things You Can Do by the Seashore*
Copyright © 2003 by Jim and Joanne Hubal

Published by
Marlowe & Company
An Imprint of Avalon Publishing Group Incorporated
161 William Street, 16th Floor
New York, NY 10038

Nothing in this book is intended as professional medical or psychological advice,
and none of its suggestions are meant to supersede the guidance of a
qualified medical or psychological professional.
Check with your own qualified professional as appropriate.

Library of Congress Cataloging-in-Publication Data
Hubal, Jim.
A week at the beach : 100 life-changing things you can do by the seashore /
by Jim and Joanne Hubal.
p. cm.
ISBN 1-56924-491-X
1. Beaches—Recreational use. 2. Outdoor recreation. 1. Hubal, Joanne. II. Title.
GV191.6.H83 2003
796'.083—dc21   2003041271

9   8   7   6   5   4   3   2   1

Designed by Pauline Neuwirth, Neuwirth & Associates, Inc.

Printed in Canada
Distributed by Publishers Group West

To our parents, Quent and Val Junger,

and Vic and Betty Hubal,

for a lifetime of support and love.

before you dive in

———

The ocean is magic. Under its spell we do things we wouldn't do anywhere else. Business suits are left behind on the cottage floor. Mothers let their children run unattended while they finish reading novels. And the poorest among us wait in line with the rich and famous to get a taste of our favorite ice cream.

This book offers a way to harness the power of the beach experience to rejuvenate, inspire, relax, challenge, and delight. From our own commutes to the seashore, we gathered 100 life-changing things to do during your beach vacation, simple activities that we found enhanced our own visits to the coast, and helped us carry the feeling of renewal and fun back home afterward.

These thought-provoking activities can be done in small snatches of time, tucked between family or social obligations, and require only materials and situations common to seaside locations. Most require no materials at all. Some activities may nudge you to rub elbows with the locals, and tap into their knowledge of the day-to-day workings of a seaside town, or the ways of the ocean.

If you like, let this book become a journal, a beach note-book, or a personal chronicle of your time together with the ocean. You'll find a space after each of the 100 suggestions for your thoughts, feelings, or doodles.

Alternating with the activities you will find 100 pieces of quirky beach trivia. We think you'll find these tidbits, quizzes, tips, and quotations informative, often surprising, and always entertaining. The broad selection of subjects provides an array of jumping off points should you wish to pursue topics that are of special interest to you.

For many of us, spending time by the ocean is a treasured experience, but we live in a world that can quickly overwhelm the best of plans with complications. This book is intended to help you rise above the practical details of life, and have the most memo-rable beach experience ever. The activities and tidbits are part sug-gestion, part challenge, and part new information. Together they will help you make every precious ocean minute count.

a week at the beach

1 Watch a sunrise. No coffee, no talking, no kids. Just you and a blanket on the beach, in the dark, waiting for the sun to shimmy out of the water or poke out from behind buildings or land. The most powerful message of all: Anything is possible today.

I've taken to chasing the light, which means rising when it is still dark and driving to the fish pier to view the fiery dawn. I'm always amazed to find others there, people who care to pay homage as one planet bows to the other, to see first a narrow pink stripe dividing water and sky, followed by a broad splash of pungent orange.

—From *A Year by the Sea*
by Joan Anderson

Beaches are places of mystery and wonder,
waiting to be explored.

—From *Ribbons of Sand: Exploring Atlantic Beaches*
by Larry Points and Andrea Jauck

2

Follow someone's footprints in the sand.
Let one set lead you to another. Was the
person wearing shoes? Did he or she run or walk? Was he or she
alone? You choose which footprints to follow.

You decide where your own footprints will lead you—and maybe
where yours will lead someone else.

3 Pick up a handful of pebbles. Think about some of the "pebbles" that are weighing you down. Each time you think of one, throw a rock out into the surf as far as you can—so far it can't possibly find its way back.

Toss as many pebbles as you need to (and maybe even a boulder or two), until you feel lighter.

fill in the beach

Fill in the beach of choice next to each famous person:

1. Henry Thoreau _____
2. Jack London _____
3. Jesus _____
4. Pablo Casals _____
5. Edgar Allen Poe _____
6. Paul Gauguin _____

Choices:

a. Georgia and South Carolina beaches

b. Cape Cod

c. South Seas

d. Sea of Galilee

e. Diamond Head (Hawaii)

f. Puerto Rico

Answers: 1/b, 2/e, 3/d, 4/f, 5/a, 6/c

—Adapted from *Beaches: Their Lives, Legends, and Lore*
by Seon and Robert Manley

who knew?

Going to the beach is the number one summer activity for nearly 180 million travelers each year. This means 179,999,999 other people plan to join you. Together we will spend nearly $640 billion by the sea.

—From the Travel Industry Association of America
and EPA statistics

4 Buy a stack of picture postcards. Choose ones that show what you're experiencing at the beach. Each day write a message on the back of one of the cards and mail it to yourself at your home or work address.

When you walk in the door back home, or sit down at your desk, pictures and words from the beach will be there to welcome you.

5

Say "Good morning" to everyone in your family every morning. Say "I love you" to everyone in your family every night. Hug each one at least once during the day.

This may be the best vacation you'll ever have.

things to see by the sea

Kilauea, one of the most active volcanoes on earth, and Mauna Loa, the world's largest volcano, are both part of Hawai'i Volcanoes National Park on the "big island" of Hawai'i. Although they still spew out tons of lava periodically, and send rivers of slow moving lava down their slopes, visitors may safely tour the crater areas and view the displays at two visitor centers in the park.

—From *America the Beautiful: Hawai'i*
by Sylvia McNair

room with a view

The Great Barrier Reef, in the Coral Sea off northeast Australia, is the largest and most spectacular collection of coral reefs in the world. . . . Tourists can stay in basic campsites, or in floating luxury hotels directly over the coral!

—From *Seas & Oceans*
by Jane and Steve Parker

6   **M**arry someone. Understandably, you may have to make some arrangements in advance. But what a setting! Perhaps you might *ask* someone to marry you, or renew your vows with your partner.

The only details that really matter are that it happens on the beach, and that neither of you wears shoes. Then every time you see the ocean, or feel sand or a mossy rock under your feet, you will remember love all over again.

7

Turn off the television.

We once saw the most disturbing sight: A man with an ocean-front room sitting on his balcony watching television, his back turned away from the spectacular dolphin display behind him.

At the beach, the greatest show on earth is just a glance away.

basic beachcombing kit

- Field notebook/sketch pad
- Pens, pencils, waterproof markers
- Ruler or tape measure
- Magnifier
- Bug box/small plastic containers
- Binoculars
- Camera
- Scoop net/bucket

—From *Discover Nature at the Seashore:
Things to Know and Things to Do* by Elizabeth P. Lawlor

the history of flip-flops

Flip-flops, those popular rubber beach shoes, are really modern versions of the traditional Japanese footwear called zori. The zori was designed so that it was easy to slip off, necessary in a country where footwear is removed before entering a house. Also known as sandals, thongs, and (in Hawai`i) *slippahs*, flip-flops are regarded by some as the most comfortable, convenient, and versatile shoes on the planet.

—From the *washedashore* web site
(*www.washedashore.com*)

8 Go for a run or walk in the surf. Even if the water is only ankle deep, you'll be surprised how much resistance it offers.

You might also be surprised at how total the experience becomes. Slipping sand, chilly water, slick rocks, soothing sounds. Just you and the ocean moving along together, each at your own pace.

9

Take a helicopter or seaplane ride, unless you're afraid of flying. Then take *two* rides.

a beachless sea?

In the middle of the western Atlantic is a relatively calm area of water known as the Sargasso Sea. Floating on the surface are thick layers of seaweed, which provide food for all sorts of small sea creatures.

In the Sargasso Sea, freshwater eels from North America and Europe come to spawn. The young eels, called elvers, are carried by the Gulf Stream toward the rivers where the adult eels came from. There they stay and feed until they make the return journey thousands of miles to the Sargasso Sea to breed.

—From *The Atlantic Ocean*
by Julia Waterlow

how to buy a lighthouse

The best sources of information on purchasing a lighthouse are the regional offices of the General Services Administration (GSA). The GSA is the Federal government's real estate broker. The GSA first offers the lighthouse property to the state or a non-profit historic preservation group; then the property may be auctioned to the highest bidder. Prospective buyers should check the GSA web site, *www.gsa.gov/regions.htm*

—From the *U.S. Coast Guard* web site
(*www.uscg.mil*)

10

Got a "to-do" list?

Pass parts of it on to others.

Make a list of all the things that have become your responsibility, even at the beach. Laundry, shopping, cooking, walking the dog, packing the car. Put each duty on a different slip of paper. Give some of those slips to others in your family or group, and ask them to do those things for you. (Maybe tomorrow you can return the favor.)

If you're alone, think about not doing anything on your list at all.

11

Wear something you have never worn before—a wild hat, a bikini, red nail polish, a beard, a nose ring (clip-on, of course). Enjoy it. You're at the beach! Other than family or friends who might have come with you, no one knows you here. You're incognito. It's not *really* you. Or is it?

jousting on rubber rafts

Two players, each holding a plastic bat, sit on rafts and try to push each other off into the water. Like the knights of long ago jousting on horseback, the one who stays mounted longest is the winner. . . . The winner may have the privilege of stretching out on his raft, relaxing, while the loser paddles him around and around the pool in a victory parade.

CAUTION: Do *not* use sharp instruments for this game.

—From *Games to Play in the Pool*
by Nancy Robison

great beach reading

- *Gift from the Sea* by Anne Morrow Lindbergh
- *Beach: Stories by the Sand and Sea,* edited by Lena Lenček and Gideon Bosker
- *A Year by the Sea* by Joan Anderson
- *The Perfect Storm* by Sebastian Junger

12

Follow the trail left by the tide. It's usually a meandering, wet path of seaweed, rocks, shells, and litter—the flotsam and jetsam of nature and people.

If you're lucky, it will lead you to a tide pool or cave. If not, it will graciously show you the way back home.

13

Walk around a candy store. Buy something you haven't eaten since you were a kid. Licorice pipes, Pixy Stix®, wax lips, Blow Pops®. As you eat it, think back and remember how good your childhood sometimes tasted.

cotton candy

A frothy, spun-sugar candy first sold in amusement parks in the 1920s. Hence any insubstantial, facilely satisfying entertainment.

—From *The NY Public Library Book of Popular Americana*
by Tad Tuleja

O.K, it's mostly sugar, but a cone of cotton candy contains only about 100 calories and less sugar than a can of regular soda. . . . In as little as two square feet of floor or counter space, you can place this easy-to-use cash generator that will continually bring in AT LEAST 90 cents profit on every dollar sold!

—From the *funprofit* web site
(*www.funprofit.com*)

removing a fishhook from your body

If the fishhook is in superficial skin, use a sterile razor blade, cut down to the shank, and lift it out. Flood the wound with antiseptic and bandage.

If the fishhook is *deeply* embedded, push the hook through the skin until the barbed end comes through. Snip off the eye end of the shank with wire cutters, then pull on the barbed end and ease out the shank. Clean and bandage.

Note: If the fishhook is in or near the eye, do not use antiseptic to clean the wound.

—From *Sea Survival: The Boatman's Emergency Manual,*
by Robb Huff and Michael Farley

14 Go fishing, crabbing, or clamming. Sign on with a pro, or find someone local to take you along for the ride. Notice the array of equipment and the special language that goes with it.

Eat what you catch. If you didn't catch anything, go to a grocery store or restaurant, buy what you should have caught, and enjoy it just the same.

15 Leave your phone at home.

It wasn't too long ago that we didn't have cell phones. It wasn't too long before that that we didn't have phones at all.

Talk to your partner. Talk to your kids. Talk to total strangers. Talk to yourself. Or don't talk at all. Listen.

it's a woman's (underwater) world

Despite the existence and use of a great deal of sophisticated underwater equipment today, free diving, as the ancients did it, is still widely practiced. This is particularly true in Japan and Korea, where colonies of women, about 30,000 of them, are employed to gather edible shellfish and seaweeds from the bottom of the sea. At one time men also engaged in this activity, but they were entirely replaced by women because female swimmers could endure the cold water better and stay submerged longer.

—From *Undersea Vehicles and Habitats:*
The Peaceful Uses of the Ocean by Frank Ross, Jr. (1970)

who knew?

An average-sized sand grain weighs only about two and a half times as much as the same volume of water, but more than two thousand times as much as an equal volume of air. This is why beach sand within reach of the tides is almost always on the move, while only the smallest sand particles are wind-borne.

—From *Tideline* by Ernest Braun

16

Take a magnifying glass to the shore. Pick up a handful of rocks, sand, shells, or seaweed and appreciate the small wonders. Can you find any signs of life? You hold a tiny world in your hand.

17

Eat a ridiculously huge ice cream cone (or as much of one as you want to). Order a cone made up of flavors you've never tried before, or pile all your favorite flavors together.

While you're eating this special cone, count the delicious minutes of enjoyment, not the calories.

tongue twisters

Say it fast

> Sally's selfish selling shellfish,
> So Sally's shellfish seldom sell.

or

> If neither he sells seashells,
> Nor she sells seashells,
> Who shall sell seashells?
> Shall seashells be sold?

—From *A Twister of Twists, A Tangler of Tongues* collected
by Alvin Schwartz

41

hands-on fishing

From March to September during spring high tides, the California Grunion spawns at night on beaches. The eggs are buried in the moist sand and hatch when the next spring tide occurs. . . . Anglers are only allowed to use their hands to capture these fishes at this time.

—From *The Audubon Society Field Guide to North American Fishes, Whales, and Dolphins* by Daniel W. Gotshall (Pacific Coast Fishes chapter)

18

Build a sand castle. Use sticks, feathers, shells, stones, buckets, and a shovel. Use your hands. Use your imagination.

When you're done with your sand castle, ask yourself what else you can build with those wonderful hands and that vivid imagination.

19

Go outside before, during, and after a storm. Watch the clouds move in, feel the wind pick up and change direction, and listen to the rain pelt the land and buildings. Afterward, look for a rainbow and know this moment is your pot of gold.

the three basic rules of boating

1. You can't ignore the weather.
2. You can't gamble against the weather.
3. You can't beat the weather.

—From *Heavy Weather Boating Emergencies*
by Chuck Luttrell

things to see by the sea

Long Beach, Washington, is home to the World Kite Museum with its rare collection of vintage kites. Each August in Long Beach, one of the nation's largest kite festivals fills the sky with brightly colored shapes while the beach buzzes with an international crowd of kite-flying enthusiasts.

—From *The Official Washington State Tourism Travel Planner*

20

Play dead. Let someone bury you in the sand.

When you feel good and dead, remember that you're not, and ask yourself: *Is there anything I'd like to do before it's too late to do it?*

21

Find a library or bookstore. Pick a letter of the alphabet, then go to the fiction shelves and check out, or buy, a book by an author whose name begins with that letter.

Or, if you'd rather, pick out a book that has your favorite color on the cover.

The important part is that you take a chance. It may turn out to be the most wonderful book you've ever read.

Water covers more than two-thirds of the earth; man had to find his way across it. And so, down through the ages, man with his ingenuity and his courage fashioned the ship—free, charged with the strength and grace and poetry of the singing sea. And where once dugout and raft, galley and galleon, tall clipper and beamy paddle-wheeler tracked the sea, now giant freighters, tankers, and liners steam in endless movement around the world, bearing man's cargoes, his hopes, himself.

—From *Men, Ships and the Sea*
by Captain Alan Villiers

who knew?

The water thrown up a beach by breaking waves is called the *swash*.
When water drains back down the beach it is called the *backwash*.

—From *Around the Coast*
by Mark C. W. Sleep

22

Sleep outdoors. If it's not allowed on the beach, then use a balcony, a deck, a patio, screened porch, or the backyard. Bring an air mattress from home, or rough it on folded blankets. No sleep you've ever had before will match it.

23

Look at the bodies on the beach. Each one is a work of art. Each one breathes, moves, and does hundreds of wondrous things. No two are alike.

Think of all the things your body does for you, and say "thanks" to it, one part at a time.

beach movies
you probably haven't seen

Beach Babes from Beyond (1993)

Girls Wrestling at the Beach (1897)

Goodrich Dirt among the Beach Nuts (1917)

Vampires on Bikini Beach (1988)

Making Love on the Beach (1898)

Beauty and the Beach (1941)

Ham at the Beach (1915)

Computer Beach Party (1988)

Psycho Beach Party (2000)

The Beach Girls and the Monster (1965)

—From *The Internet Movie Database* web site
(*www.imdb.com*)

maldive dreamin'

❖

The Maldive Islands are a tourist's dream come true. Consisting of 1,196 islands in 26 distinct coral atolls, they stretch from the south-western tip of India all the way to the Equator. This pristine tropical paradise has swaying palms, pure white sand beaches, and sparkling turquoise lagoons to lure tourists, especially divers, from all over the world. The country has developed a limited number of quality resorts, each on its own otherwise-uninhabited island, free from traffic, crime, and commercialism.

—From the *ShubhYatra* web site
(*www.shubhyatra.com*)

24 Read the want ads in the local paper. Even if your exact job isn't in the "help wanted" listings, there might be something close. Would you be willing to use another set of skills to earn a living? Could you downsize your needs if you had to? Remember the bumper sticker: *The worst day at the beach beats the best day anywhere else.*

25 Take an excursion out on the water. Go in a motorboat, paddleboat, sailboat, canoe, kayak, or rubber raft. (Even if you need to take an experienced boater or sailor with you, be sure to do some of the work yourself.)

Explore the shoreline or just drift. Look back on where you've been and feel the power of the sea beneath you.

national seashores— have you seen them all?

- 🐚 *Gulf Islands* (Mississippi/Florida)

- 🐚 *Cape Lookout* (North Carolina)

- 🐚 *Padre Island* (Texas)

- 🐚 *Cumberland Island* (Georgia)

- 🐚 *Canaveral* (Florida)

- 🐚 *Point Reyes* (California)

- 🐚 *Cape Hatteras* (North Carolina)

- 🐚 *Cape Cod* (Massachusetts)

- 🐚 *Assateague* (Maryland)

- 🐚 *Fire Island* (New York)

—From the National Park Service

what is a time-share?

Time-sharing permits multiple purchasers to buy interests in real estate, usually a resort property. Each purchaser receives the right to use the facility for a certain period of time. The owner is assessed for maintenance and common area expenses based on the amount of ownership time. Some time-sharing programs specify certain months or weeks during which the owner can use the property; others provide a rotation system. Some include a swapping privilege for the ownership period to provide variety. Typically, time-shared properties are used for 50 weeks each year, with the remaining two weeks reserved for maintenance and improvements.

—From *Modern Real Estate Practice*
by Galaty, Allaway, and Kyle

26

Write a letter to someone you've always wanted to write to, but never have. Maybe a teacher who made an impact, an old friend with whom you've lost touch, or a favorite performer. Say something positive in your letter that you have always wanted to say. It might be a fan letter, an invitation, a compliment, a love letter, or a simple "hello." Mail it.

Feel the person being touched by your letter. Feel yourself being touched by sending it.

27

Spend time under or near a pier, dock, jetty, boardwalk, or sea wall. Observe the world of plants, animals, and people who inhabit the space. Look closely in, under, and behind the space. Watch it change with the tides. Feel the rhythm of this secret world most people never notice.

test your bait I.Q.

Match the salt-water baits to the fish they catch:

1. ballyhoo   a. shark
2. bloodworm   b. bonefish
3. sand flea   c. striped bass
4. eel   d. croaker
5. yellowtail jack   e. sailfish
6. shrimp   f. snapper

Answers: 1/e, 2/d, 3/b, 4/c, 5/a, 6/f

—Adapted from *The Salt-Water Fisherman's Bible*
by Erwin A. Bauer

things to see by the sea

Willy Manchew (get it?) is a 25-foot mosquito that comes into town for the three day mosquito festival held in Clute Park in Clute Park, Texas, on the Gulf Coast. Festivities include a mosquito calling contest and a mosquito swatter decorating award. The festival is held annually the last Thursday, Friday, and Saturday in July.

—From the *tourtexas* web site
(*www.tourtexas.com*)

28

Sit next to someone who would ordinarily make you a bit uncomfortable. Maybe he or she is very good looking, or handicapped in some way, or covered with tattoos. Start a conversation with the person.

By the time you get up to leave, see if you are still uncomfortable, or if you found out the two of you weren't so different, after all.

29 Eat dinner with strangers. Do not screen them first with probing questions about jobs, education, or house size. Just choose some interesting people (on the beach towel next to you, or standing in line in the hotel lobby) and invite them.

Talk. Eat. Learn something about someone you don't know at all. Learn something about yourself in the process.

preparing fresh squid

Cut through the arms near the eyes. Squeeze out the inedible beak and reserve the tentacles. Remove the chitinous pen from inside the body mantle. Firmly grasp pen and attached viscera and remove from mantle. Wash mantle thoroughly, drain, and cut crosswise into rings. Combine boiling water, salt, squid rings and tentacles and simmer for three minutes. Add lemon peel and simmer five minutes longer.

Drain squid and serve on salad greens with vinaigrette. Garnish with parsley.

Serves six.

—From *Shellfish Heritage Cookbook*
compiled by Robert H. Robinson

set your sights

The sextant is so named because its arc approximates one-sixth of a circle. . . . The most important function of the sextant is to measure altitudes above the sea horizon. . . . The sextant shares with the compass and the chronometer the honor of being one of the three instruments that have made modern ocean navigation possible.

—From *Primer of Navigation* (third edition)
by George W. Mixter

30 Learn to tie sailors' knots, read a navigational chart, or use a sextant. Pick up a book about sailing, or check out the local marina to find a real sailor to teach you.

Once you've mastered a few skills, you will yearn to use them at sea like mariners of old. Nothing connects all the elements of the universe like sailing.

31

A*lmost* quit your job. Write a letter of resignation, but don't mail it, at least not until you've been home long enough for your tan to fade. Could any of the reasons you want to quit be turned into changes you could ask for that would make it easier to stay? Then ask for them. If there are truly irreconcilable differences, maybe it is time to move on. World's biggest beach thought: What do you want to do with the rest of your life?

who knew?

All life on earth depends on the oceans because they are the largest manufacturers of oxygen on the planet.

—From *Ocean Pollution*
by Maria Talen

going for the gold

The question about pirates burying their treasure has been much discussed. . . . There were a few who, before hitting the liberty port, were prudent enough to dig a hole and stash away part of their haul. . . . There were occasions when pirates buried their valuables before going into battle. . . . [It] is safe to say that untold fortunes were hidden quickly in rocky coves or buried on lonely beaches by roving pirates who never returned. This fact is much in evidence by the many, many 'finds'. . . .

—From *Shipwrecks, Skin Divers, and Sunken Gold*
by Dave Horner

32

Watch a single wave coming to shore. Notice how it breaks. Observe its height, and follow what it does as it spreads on the shore. Look carefully to see if your wave brought you a special gift. Be sure to give thanks if it did.

33

Whack-A-Mole. Or a frog. Or whatever pops up in this popular arcade game. If your beach has this game, play it. No matter how quick you are, no matter how hard you whack one mole down in its hole with the rubber mallet, another one always pops up to take its place. Whack-A-Mole is the quintessential metaphor for life.

bad luck onboard

Legend has it that you're bad luck for the ship if you have . . .

. . . cut your hair or fingernails

. . . killed seabirds

. . . not paid your debts

. . . committed a terrible crime

. . . recently married your godmother

. . . brought a mummy onboard

. . . led a sinful life

. . . died during the voyage

—From *Legends of the Sea*
by F. Morvan

who knew?

Gulls are found almost anywhere around the world and can live to be thirty years old. The smallest gull, the little gull, is only eleven inches long. The largest gull, the great black-backed gull, is about two and one-half feet long with a wing spread of about six feet.

—From *Gulls . . . Gulls . . . Gulls*
by Gail Gibbons

34

Find a jar with a tight lid. Scoop up sand, rocks, shells, and water and fill the jar. Shake it up on the beach and watch it settle down again.

Later on, back home, shake it up and watch *yourself* settle down again, too.

35

Attend an event unlike anything you've ever been to before. A talent contest, a fish fry at the fire hall, a presentation by a park ranger, an art show, a late-night jazz concert at a fancy restaurant, a tent revival meeting, a nature walk. If you like, let someone else do the picking, but go.

beach volleyball rules

Beach volleyball has the same rules as indoor volleyball except:

- You may go completely under the net, as long as you don't interfere with your opponent.
- Open hand, fingertip hitting is not allowed.
- The server must clearly release or toss the ball before contacting the ball on the serve.
- A player may have only one toss per serve attempt.
- When digging a hard-driven spike, it can be double hit and momentarily lifted. Open hand digs are okay.

—From the California Beach Volleyball Association

sand to go

—◆—

Take home a sand sculpture to hang on your wall. Here's how:

1. Make a box on the sand with sticks or twigs.
2. Wet the sand inside and smooth the surface.
3. Press your hand, foot, shells or whatever you wish into the sand to leave an impression.
4. Dribble wet plaster over the impressions and put in a cord or paper clip as a hanger.
5. Smooth the plaster, let dry, and remove the frame.

—From *Sand Sculpturing*
by Mickey Klar Marks

36

Stand alone on the shore and imagine you are talking to someone you miss. Tell them why you miss them, as well as anything you forgot to say before they were gone.

Feel them listening. Allow yourself to see their reaction and hear what they say back to you.

37

Talk to a lifeguard. Find out what made them become one. What was their most frightening moment? What are their plans for the future? What about this person isn't at all what you expected?

how to rescue a drowning person

Do not swim to the aid of the drowning person unless you are trained. They may pull you under. Get help right away.

Whenever possible:

- ☞ Extend your arm, leg, or any long object to the victim; even a towel may work.

- ☞ Throw a flotation device to the victim. If the device has a rope attached, pull the victim to safety.

- ☞ Row out to the victim (if you have rowing skills). Throw them a flotation device or allow the victim to hang onto the oar or stern of the boat as you row to shore. Pull the victim aboard if possible.

- ☞ Wade out to the victim, being aware of currents. If possible, extend something for the victim to grab.

—From *The American Red Cross First Aid and Safety Handbook* by American Red Cross and Kathleen A. Handal, M.D.

things to see by the sea

The beach at Rantau Abang, Malaysia, is a must-see for turtle lovers. There visitors lay in wait quietly from midnight to dawn to watch giant leatherback turtles laying eggs on the white sandy beach. Rantau Abang is one of only six places in the world visited by these turtles from the months of May to September.

—From the *Rantau Abang* web site
(*www.journeymalaysia.com/I_rantauabang.htm*)

38

Shave your head, cut your hair, get a permanent or a new color.

Be daring. It will always grow back. That's why they call it a bad hair *day*.

39

Go horseback riding. Whether you're a beginner or a seasoned rider, riding a horse near the seashore is exciting. Riding a horse *on* the seashore is as close to heaven as we dare to get.

———◆———

Whenever I walk along a sandy stretch of beach or explore a small pebbly cove, I am inevitably drawn to the shells and other remnants of sea creatures washed ashore by waves. It does not matter whether the shells are tiny or large, broken or perfectly preserved—I am always fascinated by these colorful pieces of animal architecture abandoned by their owners. As a shell collector I think of myself as the lucky inheritor of some of nature's masterpieces.

—From *Neptune's Garden: Shells A to Z*
by Wendy Frost

Clouds are sometimes described as if they were evil birds who could be fought by violent means. A Breton folk-tale tells of a voyage when the sky suddenly darkened and the sailors saw rapidly bearing down on them a cloud so dreadful to see that it struck terror into their hearts. The captain ordered the crew to shoot arrows into the center, this they all did, except for one who hit the side of the cloud, which burst, discharging such huge quantities of water onto the ship that it sank.

—From *Legends of the Sea*
by F. Morvan

40

Watch the clouds. Nowhere on earth do clouds change as quickly or dramatically as they do near the ocean. The sky can go from serenely blue to thunderheads in minutes.

The perfect cloud-watching perch is a blanket on the beach, but a comfortable chair on the porch works, too. The time-worn game of trying to see shapes in the clouds works just as well today as it did back when doing it didn't make us feel silly. How many animals can you see? Is your cousin's face at the end of that cumulonimbus?

41

Look through the trash for something cool. Beach towns are known for the great stuff thrown away or left behind.

By the Sunday afternoon exodus, the most wonderful things will be piled by the curb. Beach chairs, boogie boards, condo furniture—just about anything that won't fit in someone's car or would be of little use further inland.

Grab it, and think of it as recycling—and as just plain smart.

beach slang

beach bum: A man who frequents beaches, especially one who is a surfer, who conspicuously shows his muscles

beach bunny: A girl who, whether or not a surfer, spends time with surfers

beach blanket bingo: The love game pursued semi-nude amidst sun and sand

—From *New Dictionary of American Slang*
edited by Robert L. Chapman, Ph.D.

who knew?

—◆—

Q: Does saltwater taffy really have saltwater in it?

A: "Well, it has salt in it, and it has water in it, but not saltwater from the ocean. I think it got its name because it's made near the beach."

—From the owner of Dolle's Candyland
in Rehoboth Beach, Delaware

42

Take a nap in a hammock. Find one strung between two trees, or set up an inexpensive one purchased at a discount store.

Feel the wind work its way around you. Feel the gentle sway your movements bring. Know that you can relive some of these sensations if you set up the hammock back home—in your backyard, on your back porch, or in your living room.

43

Spell out a message on the beach. Use anything you can find—litter, twigs, rocks. Make it so large it will be visible from a low-flying plane, or so small only the most observant beach stroller could see it.

We once found a message that said "I love Mary" spelled out in the sand with the tiniest of clam shells. We wondered if the writer ever told Mary face-to-face.

just what the doctor ordered

"Dr. Beach," the alter ego of Dr. Stephen P. Leatherman, has just the prescription to help you find, enjoy, or even protect, your favorite beach. Dr. Leatherman, the director of the Laboratory for Coastal Research at Florida International University in Miami, has visited every one of this country's 650 major public beaches. He publishes lists of the best swimming, walking, wilderness, sports, city, novelty, and surfing beaches in America.

—From the *Dr. Beach* web site
(*www.drbeach.org*)

extreme surfing glossary

extreme surfing: A sport in which people ride surfboards and perform stunts on large waves

bomb: A large wave that appears suddenly

clean face: A wave face with a smooth surface

cloudbreaker: A wave that breaks far from the shore

cranking wave: A large wave that breaks quickly on a zipper

face: The side of a wave that faces the shore

gnarly wave: A wild, rough wave

zipper: A series of waves that break quickly

—From *Extreme Surfing*
by Edward Voeller

44

Go natural. Put away the hairpiece, the makeup kit, the uplift bra, the wig, the girdle. Stop shaving for a few days. Spend your vacation with the *real* you.

45 Scoop up a tablespoon of sand. Spread the grains out and look closely. Each one is unique in some way. Try to count them, then look around you on the beach and do the math. Feel humbled, but remember that everything on Earth is one of a kind.

sorry, quentin

Hurricanes are given names to avoid confusion when more than one storm is being followed at the same time. A storm is named when it reaches tropical storm strength. Separate sets of hurricane names are used for different oceans and different parts of the ocean.

For example, in the eastern Pacific, six lists of English and Spanish names are used. Each list is for a particular year. After the year is over, the same list is used six years later, with the names of any notable storms retired. No "Q" or "U" are used, since names beginning with these letters are rare.

—From *The USA Today Weather Almanac*
by Jack Williams

more great beach reading

- *The Old Man and the Sea* by Ernest Hemingway

- *The Sea Around Us* by Rachel Carson

- *Kon-Tiki* by Thor Heyerdahl

- *20,000 Leagues Under the Sea* by Jules Verne

46

During your time at the beach, don't smoke, drink, or swear. No poison in. No poison out. Breathe in sunshine, salt air, seagull sounds, and sandy feet. Breathe out gratitude, humility, gentleness, and thanks.

47

Help support the beach. Find out what beach restoration or ecological projects are going on during your visit. Take a shift guarding a shorebird nesting site from intruders, help plant dune grass, or participate in an organized clean-up event.

No matter how much we give to the beach, we can never really pay off our debt.

adopt a beach

Beach clean-up programs are alive and well all over the United States. When individuals or groups "adopt" a beach, it means they are committed to picking up and removing trash on a regular basis. Although most adopt-a-beach programs focus their efforts on spring and fall, anytime is a good time to clean up the shoreline.

Since it began in 1986, Texas Adopt-A-Beach volunteers have removed over 4,000 tons of litter from the coastal areas. Their slogan, "Don't mess with Texas beaches!," has helped raise public awareness of the importance of keeping their shoreline clean.

—From the *Texas General Land Office* web site
(*www.glo.state.tx.us*)

oceans of fun for kids

A sampling of activities at seaside camps:

- lei stringing and canoe carving

- SCUBA certification classes

- lagoon snorkeling

- photographing puffins

- petroglyph tours

- conducting marine biology experiments

- waterskiing, windsurfing, and sailing

- kayaking with seals, porpoises, and whales

Lists of camps are available from most state tourism offices and coastal chambers of commerce.

48

Play a game with someone else, or with a group. Badminton, checkers, Go Fish, croquet, Monopoly®, volleyball. If your playmate is a young child, let them choose (or make up) the game.

Some people think playing games is a waste of time. You're smart enough to know better.

49 Don't check your e-mail this week.

If that idea is too radical, ask someone else to check it for you. They can let you know if something is serious enough for you to brush the sand off your fingers and respond.

scrimshaw

———◆———

Born of the tedium that almost every whaleman felt during the idle days at sea, scrimshaw developed as a unique American art form. Whales' teeth, whalebone, walrus tusks, and even seashells served for raw material. The jackknife was the universal tool. Infinite time and patience were the artist's contribution. On the hard teeth he might engrave a ship, a girl . . . a flag, a scene of life at home or on the sea. From whalebone he might construct a basket, a birdcage, or a sewing box. Almost all the pieces were designed as presents for loved ones at home.

—From *Seafaring America*
by Alexander Laing

dead sea mud

The Dead Sea, at the foot of the Judean Hills, is the lowest spot on earth, 730 meters below sea level. Here nature is thought to have healing powers like nowhere else. A body of water with ten times the salt content of any other, numerous minerals, and a constant temperature of 38 C, it provides the ideal place to cleanse the body, relieve muscle tension and pain, and produce a deep sensation of calm.

The black Dead Sea mud is sold worldwide. Placing the mud on skin has been reported to invigorate circulation, absorb toxins, and strengthen hair.

—From an ad for Ein Gedi Resort Hotel/Spa

50

Take your lists of aches and pains—the ones your doctor couldn't help with—and visit a natural health-care clinic. See a chiropractor, an herbalist, a nutritionist, an aromatherapist, a controlled breathing instructor, or an acupuncturist. See if someone can help make your ride back home more comfortable.

51

Ask someone for a date. Romance might be one goal, but there are plenty of other ones, like learning something new. Talk to the man in the checkout line who seems to know a lot about classic cars, or the elderly woman on the next bench who has lived in this town for decades and knows everything about it. Invite them for a cup of coffee or lunch.

Or ask out your spouse or best friend as if you've just met them for the first time. Get to know them again from the very beginning.

best shelling beaches

On Captiva and Sanibel Islands in Florida are some of the richest shelling areas in the Western Hemisphere. When the first settlers reached those beaches . . . they had to wade through shells piled two and three feet high to reach the solid ground where they constructed the simplest of thatched homes.

—From *Beaches: Their Lives, Legends, and Lore*
by Seon and Robert Manley

pun in the sun

Why is the ocean angry?
> Because it has been crossed so many times.

What is an ocean?
> Where buoy meets gull.

Why did the lady jump in the ocean?
> To get a wave in her hair.

What cat lives in the ocean?
> An octopus.

—From *Biggest Riddle Book in the World*
by Joseph Rosenbloom

52 Take pictures of your favorite beach *smells*.

We have a picture of our favorite boardwalk candy shop on the wall. It *smells* great every time we walk by.

Take pictures of sounds, as well. Pretty soon your home will be filled with the beach.

53

Take a walk in the fog. With much less to look at, the sounds around you will become more distinct—a foghorn, grounded birds, the slurping of the waves, your own breathing, your feet touching the sand or rocks.

Sometimes in the muted light of fog we see things most clearly. Look carefully.

celebrate the fog

Northern California, most notably the coastal area around San Francisco, is famous for its fog, especially from June to August. The community of Pacifica has decided not only to accept this meteorological condition, but to celebrate it by hosting the Pacific Coast Fog Fest.

The Fog Fest, created in 1986, is held every year during the last weekend in September, when foggy days are over and a sunny Indian summer begins. The festival features a wide range of family activities including a "Pea Soup" making contest, and even a specialty drink called the Fog Cutter.

—From the *Pacific Coast Fog Fest* web site
(*www.pacificcoastfogfest.com*)

the perfect tan

European beaches also inspired a new seaside activity—sun worshipping. During the 1920s tanned skin became an essential component of the sexy, sporty look. Sanctioned at first by such fashion leaders as Coco Chanel, tanning became an international cult by 1930.

—From *Men and Women: Dressing the Part* edited
by Claudia Brush Kidwell and Valerie Steele

54

Find out what's underneath it all. Go snorkeling, learn to scuba dive, take a trip in a glass bottom boat, or just lie facedown in the water with a mask or goggles over your eyes. You might see a reef, exotic fish, or an underwater kelp jungle.

But even if you only see a smooth, sandy bottom, or some rocks, you'll know what's going on down there.

55

Try out the most absurd concession you can find. Take a virtual roller coaster ride. Have your picture taken in full Western dress. Squeeze into a photo booth and make faces with a friend. Try to ring the bell at the Strong Man Tower.

Sometimes things that make no sense at all give us the longest-lasting memories. And the best.

shaved ice

Shaved ice, snowball, snow cone—whatever you call it, it's that paper cup of crushed ice covered with your favorite flavored syrup.

In order to make Shaved Ice you will need:

- An ice shaver

- A block of ice (from a supplier, or make your own)

- Flavored syrups (such as strawberry shortcake, coconut, or pink bubblegum)

- Assorted cups, spoons, straws, and napkins

—From the *FlavorSnow* web site
(*www.flavorsnow.com*)

who knew?

It has been estimated there are about 5 trillion tons of salt in the world oceans. Someone figured out that if all the ocean water evaporated and the salt was spread evenly over the whole earth, the pile of salt would be as high as a fifteen-story building.

—From *Incredible Facts about the Ocean: The Restless Blue Salt Water*
by W. Wright Robinson

56

Go to your favorite beach during the off-season. Seeing the ocean without people, noise, and traffic may be very different—and perhaps even more wonderful.

Find out what the locals do for fun. Check the pulse of a slower, seashore life. Check your own pulse. Maybe off-season is the time for you to take a *real* vacation.

57

Bird-listen. Like birdwatching, but with your ears.

Those screeches and chirps are a complete language of hunger, ownership, battle, and love. How many words can you hear?

seabirds of a feather

There are over 320 kinds of seabirds in all the oceans of the world. They are expert fliers and divers, and can soar on the wind for miles without flapping their wings.

Which of these seabird groups comes to your beach?

- penguins
- puffins
- auks
- pelicans
- cormorants
- boobies
- albatross
- shearwaters
- petrels
- gulls
- terns

—From *Seabirds*
by Mark J. Rauzon

keep your shirt on

Although men commonly swam in the nude at sex-segregated areas of the beach, by the 1850s, when women joined them, codes of modesty became essential. Then, long trousers and flannel shirts were prescribed beachwear for men.

—From *Men and Women: Dressing the Part* edited by Claudia Brush Kidwell and Valerie Steele

58

Walk barefoot for a day, or at least a whole morning. See what you can learn through your feet that you couldn't learn any other way.

No shirt. No shoes. No service.

So don't go in. Stay outside and touch the world with your toes.

59

Visit a shipwreck. But first visit a local maritime museum so you know what you'll be looking at. Then go on a dive to get a closer look.

Afterward, if you like, rent a metal detector and hunt for artifacts on the beach. Maybe you'll take home a piece of history—a tangible reminder of people who navigated these waters before you.

how to become a lighthouse keeper

Many lighthouses have been turned over to the National Park Service or to the various states. Some permit volunteers to staff their lighthouses. For additional information contact:

www.usalights.com

The United States Lighthouse Society
244 Kearney Street, 5th Floor
San Francisco, CA 94108
(415) 362-7255
www.maine.com/lights/uslhs.htm

a bed and breakfast innkeeper's day

7 A.M. to 10:30 A.M.

Start coffee, prepare breakfast, straighten up porch, set tables, set up juice and coffee bar, sweep, bake bread and coffee cakes, greet guests, serve breakfast, start first dishwasher load.

10:30 A.M. to 3 P.M.

Clear breakfast dishes, unload dishwasher, start second dishwasher load, clean and straighten guest rooms, do first load of laundry, clean bathrooms and kitchen, set tables for afternoon tea, check out guests, do second load of laundry, check in new guests.

3 P.M. to 10 P.M.

Prepare and serve afternoon tea, set up evening coffee, cake, and sherry; shop for groceries for tomorrow, put away all laundry and dishes, complete all office work.

—From Vivian and Bob Barry, Innkeepers
at Barry's Gull Cottage, Dewey Beach, Delaware

60

Check into owning your own beachside bed and breakfast. Many innkeepers are happy to share their expertise with others, and they can start you thinking about whether or not you have what it takes. Do you have the right finances, people skills, and energy? Ask about inn sitting or being an innkeeper's intern to learn the ropes first-hand.

"Hello, welcome to the (Your Name Here) *Bed and Breakfast. May I help you?"*

61

Go to a toy store. Buy something you always wanted as a child, but for whatever reason never owned. It's not too late to have it now. And it's never too late to play.

how to make s'mores

S'mores are a traditional beach campfire treat. They are sandwiches of marshmallow and melted chocolate bars between two graham crackers.

Put the ingredients together, wrap them in foil, and melt them over an open fire—or set them on a surface *near* (not in) a fire. A s'more can also be made quickly by setting a toasted marshmallow directly on a piece of chocolate bar already on a graham cracker. Add the top cracker and eat.

—From an old scouting recipe

synchonize your watches

Exploring Kachemak [Alaska] Bay's tide pools is the best way to really get to know the sea and meet the strange and wonderful animals that live in it, and it doesn't cost anything but the price of a pair of rubber boots. Extralow tides [some 25 feet below the high] expose more of the lower intertidal zone that contains the most interesting creatures . . . but keep track of time: The tide will come in faster than you imagine, and you could get stranded and quickly drown in the 40 degree water.

—From *Frommer's 2000 Alaska*
by Charles P. Wohlforth

62 Listen to the sand singing.

On many beaches, sand against sand makes a distinctive sound. Turn your ear away from the crash of the waves, and see if the sand on your beach is playing a song.

Sometimes the wind sings back-up while it weaves its way through the rocks and trees. Add the screech of birds and you have a symphony. All you have to do is stand on a dune and conduct.

63

Float facedown in the water. Use a rubber raft—or just take a deep breath, flop down in the water, and float until you're out of air.

Just let yourself bob on the waves. Don't paddle. The water will rub your belly. The sun will warm your back. You will become a sunshine sandwich.

removing smell from a shell

1. Make sure the entire animal is removed from the shell. (If you're not sure, place the shell in water for two weeks, changing the water every day.)
2. Place the shell into a solution of baking soda and water for one hour.
3. Rinse with water and let dry.

Other methods of cleaning shells may include boiling, freezing, hanging, or rotting (allowing the insides to decay naturally).

—From *Shellcraft Secrets*
by Greg and Shelley Stahly

dolphin facts

- There are about 40 kinds of dolphins.

- Dolphins are found in oceans throughout the world, as well as in some rivers.

- Dolphins can swim 30 miles an hour, jump 20 feet in the air, and dive 1,000 feet deep.

- A dolphin breathes air through a blowhole in the top of its head.

- Dolphins are mammals and give milk to their young.

—From *Animal World: Dolphins*
by Donna Bailey

64 Follow a dolphin, spy on a seal, watch a whale, or listen to a sea lion. You can go with a group, or find them on your own.

Leave your watch behind; when you're in their company, time stops.

65

For a day—or for your entire stay at the beach—don't use your car. Go everywhere on foot. Or rent a bicycle, Rollerblade™ in-line skates, a skateboard, or a scooter. With all these possibilities, who needs a car?

the beach week that never ends

Lucky homeowners on the world's first residential resort community at sea, the World of ResidenSea, will live in one of 110 luxurious shipboard apartments (up to 3,200 square feet), play tennis and golf, eat at world class restaurants, and attend concerts, all while continuously circumnavigating the globe. Apartment owners can go ashore for the Cannes Film Festival, then back "home" onboard the ship for a visit to the spa before cruising through the Chilean fjords. Units priced from $2,000,000.

—From the *ResidenSea* web site
(*www.residensea.com*)

nothing shifty here

And everyone that heareth these sayings of mine, and doeth them not, shall be likened unto a foolish man, which buildeth his house upon the sand; And the rain descended, and the floods came, and the winds blew and beat upon that house; and it fell: and great was the fall of it.

—Matthew 7:26–27

According to beach engineers, Matthew's statement is accurate—for the desert. The desert sand is always dry and shifting.

But the damp, contained sand of the seashore is firm enough to hold buildings and even roads. The timber pilings holding up many beach homes are not used because the sandy soil will wash away, but to keep the houses elevated above floodwaters.

66

Read an inspirational or spiritual book all
the way through.

This doesn't have to be a book about a specific religion or idea. In
fact, for the most thought provoking results, pick a topic you
know little about. Or do the opposite, and read once again the
inspirational or spiritual book that has moved you the most, or
had the greatest effect on your life.

The seashore has an uncanny knack for making new ideas and
understandings flow gently over the rockiest of shores.

67

For one hour pick up every piece of litter you see on the beach. Do people say "thank you" when they see what you're doing? Do others start to bend over and pick up litter, too?

You've become a positive role model. Keep up the good work.

lobster links

When spiny lobsters migrate in the autumn, they form lines and march in single file across the ocean floor. Each creature stays in contact with the one in front. If an enemy appears the lobsters back away from it and point their spiny antennae in an attack position.

—From *Under the Sea* edited
by Dr. Frank H. Talbot

things to see by the sea

P. T. Barnum made Bridgeport, Connecticut, the headquarters for "The Greatest Show on Earth." The Barnum Museum is housed in a Romanesque Revival building (961 Main Street) built by the showman in 1890. Exotic exhibits such as a model of a circus with half a million figures are on display. Barnum and his most famous attraction, General Tom Thumb, are buried in Bridgeport at Mountain Grove Cemetery.

—From *The Smithsonian Guide to Historic America*
(Southern New England), text by Henry Wiencek

68

During your time at the beach, record your dreams. Keep paper and a pencil or pen by your bedside. You may discover that vacation dreams are different from work-week dreams.

Even if it's just a few words at first, write down what you can remember when you first awaken. Once you tell your mind to pay attention while you are busy sleeping, it will do its job well. Some things work better if we step aside and let nature take over.

69

For one day—or for a week—don't look in a mirror. Do whatever you usually do to your face by feel, or don't do it at all.

Do others around you see a difference? Do you see a difference in how others look at you? But you won't know whether or not you actually look different because (remember?) you aren't going to look in the mirror.

who knew?

Peruvians call the warm Pacific current El Niño ("The Child") because
it usually arrives around Christmas, but it is nothing to celebrate.
The heat of El Niño kills or drives away schools of fish that fishermen
depend on. Sometimes so many fish die that their rotting bodies
turn ships' paintwork black.

—From *The Pacific Ocean*
by David Lambert

sailboat maintenance 101

The water entering a cored [sailboat] deck cannot get back out; the flow is one way, like filling a jug. Balsa cores become saturated and mushy. Plywood soon rots. In both cases, the only solution is cutting away the fiberglass skin and replacing the core. After you do this job once, knowing full well that it could have been prevented with four-bits' worth of caulk and an hour's worth of effort, you will become religious about maintaining a watertight seal around any hole in the deck.

—From *Sailboat Hull & Deck Repair*
by Don Casey

70

Read a comic book. Browse the shelves and see what's new, or look for your childhood favorites. Buy a handful and find just the right spot to read.

Share your comics with your own child or grandchild, if you wish—or show them how much more exciting the stories seem if you read them under the covers with a flashlight.

71

Write something just for fun: keep a journal, write a poem, make up a play or story about the people on the next beach towel. Or let the simple objects (shells, litter, driftwood, lost toys) you find on the beach connect you to your thoughts, feelings, and memories; then write them down.

If all else fails, turn your ear toward the ocean. It is never at a loss for words.

sea temperatures

The water temperature at the surface of the sea varies from between 28 degrees F in the Arctic Ocean to 97 degrees F in the Persian Gulf. The highest temperatures anywhere in the oceans are at underwater hydrothermal vents (black smokers), where the water spurts out at over 750 degrees.

—From *Seas & Oceans*
by Jane and Steve Parker

links to the beach : clothing optional

Nude beach guide:
www.nudebeachguide.com

Nude yacht vacations:
www.nopockets.com

Nude travel and beaches:
www.bareaffairs.com

—From the 4nudistlinks web site
(www.4nudistlinks.com)

72

Get a massage. Let someone hold your body in their hands and guide your muscles to a peaceful place. Let their warm fingers lift the weight of the world from your shoulders, and remove the tension and stress you can't reach on your own.

73

Don't speak for an hour, an afternoon, a day.

At first you'll hear the beach sounds—birds, people, motorboats, waves. Keep listening until you can hear the inside of you—your breathing, your beating heart, your thoughts, your memories, your dreams. Listen closely. You have a lot to say.

Painting by the sea is a tough job, as the ocean isn't at all coopera-
tive and sometimes seems violently antagonistic. However, it is surely
worth the trouble if you are able to capture some of the grandeur
and beauty of the sea in your canvas. So think nothing of it if your
canvas blows away or you get washed off a rock. To the marine
painter, this is all good, clean fun.

—From *Painting Surf and Sea*
by Harry R. Ballinger

for more information, contact...

Oceanic Society (protection and wise use of oceans)
1536 16th Street NW
Washington, DC 20036
(800) 326-7491
www.oceanic-society.org

The Cousteau Society, Inc. (environmental education)
930 W. 21st Street
Norfolk, VA 23517
(800) 441-4395
www.cousteausociety.org

Greenpeace (ocean and wildlife preservation)
1436 U Street SW
Washington, DC 20009
(202) 462-1177
www.greenpeaceusa.org

74

W ho's across the sea? Take a look.

Someone on a faraway shore is looking back, being inspired by the same view. Reach out with both hands in their direction and know that someone somewhere is reaching back.

75

Fly a kite on the beach. Then take it home with you. Hang it where you can look at it and hear it say, "Soon we will play at the seashore again. I promise."

peter planned a perfect picnic

1. The perfect beach picnic begins with planning (keep it simple) and packing (keep it cold—40 degrees F or under for perishables).
2. Find your favorite spot—preferably away from trash containers and their resident flies and bees.
3. Put coolers under an umbrella, cover them with a blanket, or partially bury them in sand to help keep them cool.
4. Pitch perishables if they've been out in warm temperatures for over two hours—one hour when it's above 90 degrees.

—From "Food Safety at the Beach," an article by Barbara O'Brien in *Food News for Consumers*, U.S. Department of Agriculture

coldwater surfing in norway

Norway is the land of the Vikings, but is also the land of a handful of hardcore surfers. With its black, cold water, and frozen air, it's home of what I guess must be the most stoked surfers in the world. Just getting wax for the cold conditions is a problem, not to mention just staying warm and being able to move in 7 mm wetsuits.

But we have unbelievable nature with clean water and breathtaking scenarios, no thieves on the beach and almost no crowd to make up for the negatives. And when it comes to skiing, we are the best in the world!

—From an unidentified Norwegian surfer on the *onestopsurf* web site
(*www.onestopsurf.co.uk*)

76

Take a binocular walk. Find distant objects—a dune, a ship, an island, a lighthouse. Walk (or row, or sail) toward it. Things seen from a long way off can be further away than we think.

When you finally get there, is it what you thought it would be, or more?

77

Smile at everyone you see. *Everyone.*

Researchers tell us that smiling releases positive endorphins—happy hormones—into your system.

And if you really mean it, even more good things will happen.

things to see by the sea

Ride the Cyclone at Coney Island. Built in 1927, during the "Golden Age of Roller Coasters," this classic boasts 3,000 feet of track, 6 fan turns, 9 drops (the big one is 85 feet high) and a speed of up to 60 miles per hour. The Cyclone is located on Surf Avenue in Coney Island's Astroland Amusement Park, Brooklyn, New York. (The original Nathan's Hot Dogs is right next door.)

—From *The World's Wildest Roller Coasters*
by Michael Burgan

one . . . two . . . three, dip

The sea was a place to improvise and explore. It offered not only new occasions for aimless fun, but also opportunities for transposing land-based activities to water. Surf-dancing was a case in point. The rage for the waltz and the polka at some of the more fashionable resorts instantly spread to the surf, where couples performed intricate maneuvers that allowed for considerable love play. . . . As this new activity gained in popularity, many of the hotels set aside certain times for surf-dancing, and ran up a red flag to announce that the beach had been reserved exclusively for this use.

—From *The Beach: The History of Paradise on Earth*
by Lena Lencek and Gideon Bosker

78

Go dancing. Square dancing, line dancing, ballroom dancing, clogging, or something you make up on the spot. Grab your partner or meet a new one when you get there.

For a new twist, do your dancing in the sea. Wade out and boogie with the beach, either with someone else or on your own.

79

Give away some money. Drop money in the collection jar for a local shelter. Contribute to a church or synagogue. Buy a ticket to a benefit. Overtip a waiter. Pay a street musician handsomely, or surprise a beginning painter with your support of their efforts. Or simply give someone in your own family enough to buy something they want. No strings attached.

correct windsurfing position

1. Keep your arms at full stretch, your hands a shoulder-width apart.
2. Use a reverse grip with your mast hand.
3. Lean a long way out to windward.
4. Keep your spine slightly flexed, never straight or concave.
5. Slightly bend your forward leg; bend your rear leg to steer and stabilize.
6. Twist your body slightly toward the front.

—From *Perfect Windsurfing*
by Ernstfried Prade

europe's best swimming spots

The Foundation for Environmental Education in Europe publishes an annual list of the cleanest places to swim.

France had the highest number of such beaches (399), followed by Spain (390), Greece (318), Denmark (176), Portugal (115) and Italy (98). Germany had only 26 sea beaches approved, but the country has a relatively short coastline, a spokesman for the organization noted.

—From *The Dallas Morning News* web site
(*www.dallasnews.com*)

80

Take candles to the night beach. Spread out a towel and surround yourself with flickering light.

Breathe slowly and deeply. Let the sounds of the waves wash over you. Watch the candlelight struggle against the breeze. Count the stars and smile back at the moon.

81

Watch a child playing near the shore. Then do everything he or she does for fifteen minutes.

Did the child in you have fun?

beauty at the beach

Each October coastal California welcomes a group of western migrating Monarch butterflies drawn to winter roosts in pine and eucalyptus groves. In Pacific Grove, black and orange signs warn, "Butterfly Zone," and there is a $1,000 fine for molesting butterflies.

At the same time, Monarchs from the Eastern United States color the air orange and black in Cape May, New Jersey, as they gather for their journey to Central Mexico over 2,000 miles away.

—From "Monarchs," an article by Tom Horton
in *Coastal Living* magazine

One stormy autumn night when my nephew Roger was about twenty months old I wrapped him in a blanket and carried him down to the beach in the rainy darkness. Out there, just at the edge of where-we-couldn't-see, big waves were thundering in, dimly seen white shapes that boomed and shouted and threw great handfuls of froth at us. Together we laughed for pure joy—he a baby meeting for the first time the wild tumult of Oceanus, I with the salt of half a lifetime of sea love in me. But I think we felt the same spine-tingling response to the vast, roaring ocean and the wild night around us.

—From *The Sense of Wonder*
by Rachel L. Carson

82

Follow the night sounds: people eating and laughing in the open air, a dog barking his message to the world, shore birds settling down for the night, crickets and frogs singing in a marsh.

Follow the sounds wherever they lead. Then sit and quietly listen to the world of the sea after dark.

83

Take your dog to the beach, if regulations allow it, and watch your dog experience the seashore. Experience the joy of watching an uninhibited creature play and explore.

There are dead things to smell, water to swim in, sticks to retrieve, sand to dig in, and crabs to wonder about. If you can get your dog to stand still long enough, check his face for a smile and smile back.

batter up !

The popular beach treat, funnel cake, is neither a funnel nor a cake.
The traditional Amish treat gets its name because the batter is
swirled from a funnel into hot oil to create a circular "waffle" that
can be topped with powered sugar, fruit, syrup, or whipped cream.

To make funnel cake batter mix 3–4 cups flour, 3 eggs, 2 cups milk, ¼
cup sugar, 2 tsp. baking powder, and ½ tsp. salt. Drop into oil heated
to 375° F. When both sides are golden brown, remove, top,
and eat.

—From the *BerksWeb* Pennsylvania Dutch web site
(*www.berksweb.com/pam*)

the history of the bikini

The bikini was invented in 1946 and named after the Bikini Atoll, in the Marshall Islands, the site of atomic bomb testing. The inventors were two Frenchmen, Jacques Heim and Louis Reard. . . . The modern term "bikini" for a particular bathing suit design was first used by Heim and Reard. . . . Heim was a couturier designer from Cannes, France, who had designed very small bathing suits called "Atome " (French for atom). He hired a skywriting plane to advertise his design by skywriting "Atome—the world's smallest bathing suit." Three weeks later, Reard, a mechanical engineer, had another skywriting plane write "Bikini—smaller than the smallest bathing suit in the world."

—From the *Inventors with Mary Bellis* web site
(*www.inventors.about.com*)

84

Get on a local bus and ride. No destination—just ride and look. Some seaside communities have trolleys, gondolas, surreys, or rickshaws for hire. Those are fine, too. Check out the beach scene from the passenger's seat.

85 Embarrass your kids. Why not? They've been doing it to us grown-ups for years.

We saw two teenagers with their shirts pulled over the faces, screaming to their mother to "make him stop." Nearby, dad sat in an arcade "electric chair," screaming like a lunatic as the bells rang and whistles blew. But he wouldn't stop. And his wife couldn't hear her children's pleas over the sound of her own laughter.

Not more than fifteen minutes later, we saw a mother reduce her children to tears of laughter as she strutted around the beach with a circle of seagull feathers stuck in her headband.

So put on that Speedo®, plug in the karaoke machine, and get ready for the talent contest at the bandstand. Just don't tell your kids ahead of time that you're in the show.

in rain, or sleet, or whitewater

Oregon's only mail boats still deliver the U.S. mail to the remote villages. The mail deliveries began in 1895 to meet the needs of remote settlers and miners living in the Rogue River Canyon. Today, visitors to Oregon can ride along on "Postman's Run" (a 64 mile trip), the "Special Delivery" (80 miles), or the longer "Handle With Care" (104 miles) adventure.

—From the *Oregon Mail Boat* web site
(*www.mailboat.com*)

oyster eating tips

❧ The oyster shell should be tightly closed, not gaping.

❧ The oyster should be plump and cream-colored.

❧ Oysters should be served on the *deep* side of the half-shell.

❧ Freshly shucked oysters should be eaten as soon as possible
for best flavor.

—From *The Chesapeake Bay Fish & Fowl Cookbook*
by Joan and Joe Foley

86 Find one special shell or rock. Even if you've picked up buckets full, choose just one to take home and keep near you.

Only you will know why it is special. Only you will experience the calm it brings. And if you think all shells and rocks are alike, think about this: On a beach covered with thousands of small shells, we found one with a drawing of two men on the underside. Beneath the drawing were the words "Carlos y Mateo—2001."

87 Let a child take pictures for you.

Buy a disposable camera and give it to a child. Let them take pictures of whatever they want, wherever they want. If you don't have a child, grandchild, niece, or nephew with you at the beach, ask to borrow a child from a friendly family. Let them take a few pictures of you, or the beach, or both.

When you get home, blow up your favorite photographs to poster size and hang them on the wall. Then, anytime you want, you can see what the seashore looks like through the eyes of a child.

When I was a boy, about eight or nine years old, I desperately wanted a sailboat, but couldn't afford one. So I did the next best thing, I built an imaginary boat on top of a high sand dune overlooking the ocean. I outlined a boat about fifteen feet long in the sand, and hollowed out the inside. Then, using a long pole, two pieces of bamboo, and a large square of old canvas, I fashioned a square sail that caught the wind and filled beautifully. I confess I sat for hours in that sandy "boat," and I know that no sailor ever sailed as many places in as short a time as I did. Despite the many different types of boats I've sailed since then, I'll always remember how thrilled I was when that threadbare old piece of canvas filled and started to pull on the lines in my hands.

—The *Complete Beginner's Guide to Sailing*
by A. H. Drummond, Jr.

saltwater cures

Early Romans soaked their aching muscles in salt water and this notion has proved to be true. A study by the Soroka Medical Center in Israel found that patients with rheumatoid arthritis improved dramatically after daily immersion in the Dead Sea bath salts. More recently, salt soaks have been used to cure sweaty feet. Why? Because when saltwater comes in contact with skin cells, it tends to suck the water out of them. The cells tend to shrivel and dry up.

—From *The Prevention How-To Dictionary of Healing Remedies and Techniques*
edited by John Feltman

88 Cry.

The sea will give you privacy. On one side the deep ocean keeps intruders away. On the other side, sand and rocks give you fair warning if anyone approaches. The crash of the waves and howl of the wind mean no one can hear a sound you make.

During the experiences (some joyful, some not) of our many years together, neither of us cried. Not until we walked by the ocean. Alone.

89

Visit a local real estate office. Find out what it would cost to rent or buy a home near the beach. It may be more possible than you think.

A few years ago we quit our jobs, rented out the family home, and moved with our youngest child, a dog, and a cat to a condo just steps away from the ocean. And we did it without winning the lottery or saving up a giant nest egg. Maybe you can, too.

shellfish americans love to eat

American lobster: found on the eastern coast of North America, from Cape Hatteras to southern Labrador.

American oyster: found from Brazil, northward through the Caribbean and Gulf of Mexico, to the Saint Lawrence River.

Blue crab: found in the Chesapeake Bay, south Atlantic, and Gulf states.

Common shrimp: found along the Atlantic coast, Virginia to Texas and Brazil.

Snow crab: found in the North Atlantic, North Pacific from Alaska to Northern California.

Eastern surf clam: found from Maine to South Carolina.

—From *Let's Go Fishing for Shellfish*
by George Travis

tips for beach driving

General rules where driving is permitted:

1. Enter and leave the beach only at designated ramps.

2. Drive only between the ocean and dunes.

3. Follow the standard speed of 25 mph or less.

Other tips include:

1. Decrease your tire pressure to 20–25 pounds for sand.

2. Do not spin your wheels to dig out if you're stuck.

3. Park above the high tide line.

—From the *Outer Banks Beach Guide* web site
(*www.outer-banks.nc.us*)

90

Draw something. Draw right in this book,
or buy a sketch pad or blank book.

How you see things at the beach is different from how you see things back home. And how you see things *anywhere* is different from how you'd say it in words.

91

Take a walk on the shore, but keep your eyes on the shoreline (on houses, trees, and hills). Then walk back, but keep your eyes on the beach beneath your feet (on sand, rocks, and shells). Finally, take another walk on the shore, but keep your eyes on the water (on waves, clouds, ships, and seals). When you put the pieces back together, you will have 360 degrees of heaven.

how clean is your beach?

To find out if your favorite beach is on the official clean beach list, check out the Clean Beaches Council at *www.cleanbeaches.org.* This non-profit beach certification program, called the Blue Wave Campaign, helps the public identify clean and safe beaches when planning vacations.

who knew?

Pirate means "someone who plunders the sea," but there were really several different kinds. Privateers were sea raiders with a government license to pillage enemy ships. Buccaneers were 17th century pirates who menaced the Spanish in the Caribbean. Corsairs were privateers and pirates who roved the Mediterranean.

Women who dreamed of sailing the seas under the Jolly Roger had to dress, fight, drink, and swear like men. Among those who did were Anne Bonny, Charlotte De Berry, Ching Shih, "the terrible" Alvilda, and Mary Read.

—From *Pirate*
by Richard Platt

92

Consider adopting a pet and taking it home with you.

If you've thought about it carefully (and discussed it with your family), and if your lifestyle back home can provide a safe, loving, playful place for your new friend, then a vacation may be a great time to choose a pet.

Visit the local shelter and make your choice, then board your new pet at a local vet. While it's getting its shots, being neutered or spayed, and recovering, you can visit and begin to bond.

When you both leave for home, you'll be ready for a new life together.

93

Make a wish and write it in the sand with a feather. Let the next wave carry your feather out to sea. If it comes back to shore, some people believe the wish will come true.

If the feather never returns, some people believe they will get even *more* than they wished for.

the uncommon dune

Dunes by the water are found all over the world, and consist of different materials. Quartz is the most common dune material; although there are clay dunes on the Gulf Coast of Texas and calcium dunes in the Bermudas. There are even sand dunes on the south coast of Alaska and on the Arctic island, Greenland.

—From *Shifting Sands: The Story of Sand Dunes*
by Ramona Maher

buying fresh fish

Fresh Fish: Have clear, bulging eyes; elastic, firm flesh; reddish pink gills; are free from strong odor. Buy fish stored and displayed on crushed ice . . . just before using. (The fresher the better.)

—From *Betty Crocker's Picture Cook Book*
(1950 edition)

94

Eat local. Eat fresh. Not just your favorite pizza, but regional specialties and whatever else the locals eat. And don't just sample the seafood. Look for a local brewery, winery, or bakery.

Driving a few miles inland can open up new worlds of wonderful tastes. Buy fresh veggies and fruit from a farmers' market, a produce stand, or the back of a produce truck. Scarf down locally smoked fish and homemade jellies or jams, relishes, and pickles.

Take some of your favorites back home with you, and arrange to have more of them shipped to your home (if possible) long after your vacation is over.

95

Buy the wackiest or tackiest souvenir you can find. Be sure it makes you laugh.

Once you get home, put it where you can see it every day—on top of your computer, or near your toothbrush. It will be a reminder that life doesn't always have to be so serious.

and a side of seaweed, please

Seaweed is filled with vitamins and a mineral called iodine. It is a common food in countries like China and Japan. Seaweed can be eaten raw in salad or cooked as a vegetable. Seaweed soup is popular in Japan. In Wales, a red seaweed is used to make a special kind of dish called laver bread.

—From *Fascinating Facts about the Seashore*
by Jane Walker

world's most famous ship disasters—
what went wrong?

A. The Titanic (1912) _____

B. The Birkenhead (1852) _____

C. The Cospatrick (1874) _____

D. The Morro Castle (1934) _____

E. The Andrea Doria (1956)_____

—Adapted from *Ships Through the Ages*
by Douglas Lobley

96

Send a message in a bottle. Seal it tight and toss it out to sea.

It could sink and never reach anyone, or it could float for thousands of miles and change the life of whoever finds it and reads your message. Imagine the ending you want for your bottle, and for you.

97

During your last day at the beach, listen to music during a walk on your favorite section of beach. Listen to whatever will bring you back to this place: classical, jazz, oldies.

What you see and what you listen to won't necessarily match, but the music will provide a sound track for your memory. Soak up the ocean with your eyes, and see it all over again when you hear the same music back home.

music to your eyes

Along this [Oregon] coast, and northward, stretch the unmatched driftwood beaches—mammoth logs and root tangles abraded by wind, salt, and wild surf into silvery, surreal sculptures. Jostling masses of seals and sea lions blanket rocks and beaches. In the spring a rush of flowers brushes the offshore islands with color; nesting colonies settle in and the small, sharp cries of thousands of baby birds begging for food mingle with the ceaseless sounds of the surf. . . . Bold headlands bear the brunt of waves rolling in unimpeded from Asia; the sea batters itself into spray sometimes a hundred feet high, bursting through gaps and blowholes of its own making.

—From *America's Seashore Wonderlands* edited by Donald J. Crump
(Chapter 1: The Northwest by Cynthia Russ Ramsay)

starting a matchless fire

Method #1: Make a bow that revolves on a spindle in a shallow notch in a board fast enough to create a spark.

Method #2: Strike a flint sharply against steel to make a spark.

Method #3: Hold a magnifying glass at a right angle to the sun and move it back and forth to pinpoint light on tinder.

—From the *Complete Book of Outdoor Lore*
by Clyde Ormond

98

Build a fire on the beach—laws and weather permitting. If you can, use driftwood and leaves. Consider testing your survival skills by trying to start it without matches or a lighter. Cook your dinner on it—or just make popcorn or s'mores.

After a while you might catch yourself thinking, "Maybe modern life isn't so hard after all."

99

Create a beach capsule. On the last day of your stay, choose at least three items that say something important about your visit. If they are natural objects, you could bury them in the sand, or leave them near a good sitting rock for someone else to find. Otherwise you can fill a jar, or even a sandwich bag, with small mementos to take home with you.

What do you think finding those objects in the sand might mean to a stranger? What will finding them in your special place back home mean to you?

The tide rises, the tide falls
The twilight darkens, the curlew calls;
Along the sea-sands damp and brown
The traveller hastens toward the town,
And the tide rises, the tide falls.

—From "The Tide Rises, The Tide Falls"
by Henry Wadsworth Longfellow

Perhaps this is the most important thing for me to take back from beach-living: simply the memory that each cycle of the tide is valid; each cycle of the wave is valid; each cycle of a relationship is valid. And my shells? I can sweep them all into my pocket. They are only there to remind me that the sea recedes and returns eternally.

—From *Gift from the Sea*
by Anne Morrow Lindbergh

100

Watch a sunset. Alone. No wine, no children. Soak it in and let it hide behind your eyelids. Wrap it up to open later, away from the seashore, when life becomes cold, and damp, and dark. Then you'll close your eyes and let the sunset drop like a window shade and drape its warm color across the memory you now call home.

We hope that the ideas and information in *A Week at the Beach* truly helped you "make every ocean minute count." Whether you used our suggestions, or made up some of your own, we'd love to hear from you. Write us at either of the addresses below, or visit our web site, *www.JimJoBeach.com*.

Jim and Joanne Hubal

P.O. Box 1014

Rehoboth Beach, DE 19971

JimJoBeach@aol.com